SCOTTISH
SPCA

ANNUAL SCHOOLS PRIZE
COMPETITION

THE BOARD OF DIRECTORS
OF THE SOCIETY HAS GREAT
PLEASURE IN PRESENTING
THIS BOOK PRIZE TO:-

HANNAH   MIEDEMA

DK

A DORLING KINDERSLEY BOOK

Project editor Christiane Gunzi **Project art editor** Val Wright Heneghan

Editorial assistant Deborah Murrell **Designer** Julie Staniland
Design assistant Nicola Rawson

Production Louise Barratt
Illustrations Nick Hall, Nick Hewetson, Dan Wright
Additional editorial assistance Jill Somerscales

Managing editor Sophie Mitchell
Managing art editor Miranda Kennedy

Consultants
Barry Clarke, Andy Currant,
Theresa Greenaway, Paul Hillyard, Judith Marshall,
Tim Parmenter, Edward Wade, Kathie Way

First published in Great Britain in 1992 by
Dorling Kindersley Limited
9 Henrietta Street
Covent Garden
London WC2E 8PS

A CIP catalogue for this book is available from the British Library.
ISBN 0 86318 773 0

Colour reproduction by Colourscan, Singapore
Printed and bound in Italy by New Interlitho, Milan

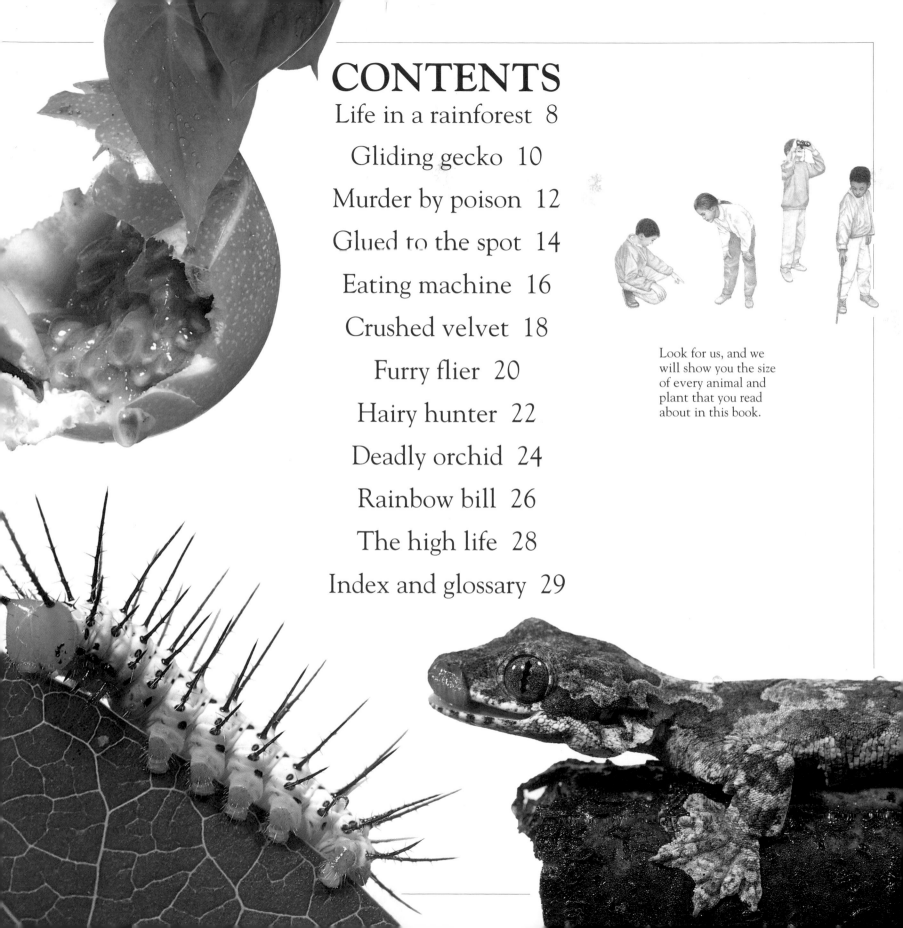

CONTENTS

Look for us, and we will show you the size of every animal and plant that you read about in this book.

LIFE IN A RAINFOREST

AN ASTONISHING VARIETY of wildlife leaps, flies, or crawls in the damp, shady world of the rainforest. Most of the animals live high up in the trees, where there is more sunlight and rain. Leaves, twigs, rotten wood, and animal droppings fall to the forest floor, where hundreds of different smaller creatures scuttle or slither around. Many rainforests have been cut down for timber, or to clear the land for farms and factories. We need to protect the forests that are left for the sake of the animals and plants that live there.

Flying gecko
Ptychozoon kuhli
10 cm long

Orchid
Odontoglossum laeve
flowers 3.5 cm wide

Orchid mantis
Hymenopus coronatus
6 cm long

Postman butterfly
Heliconius melpomene
2.5 cm long

Passion flower
Passiflora caerulea
flowers 7 cm wide

Orchid
Encyclia pentotis
flowers 5 cm wide

Postman caterpillar
Heliconius melpomene
2.5 cm long

Tiger centipede
Scolopendra gigantea
24 cm long

Cuvier's toucan
Ramphastos cuvieri
beak 12 cm long

Franquet's fruit bat
Epomops franqueti
wingspan 36 cm

White's tree frog
Litoria caerulea
6 cm long

Curly-haired tarantula
Brachypelma albopilosa
8 cm long

Poison dart frog
Dendrobates truncatus
2 cm long

GLIDING GECKO

THE FLYING GECKO lives high up in the rainforest trees. This lizard does not really fly, but its body has adapted so that it can glide from tree to tree to escape danger. Flying geckos are active mainly at night, when it is cooler. Their excellent eyesight and hearing help them to find insects to eat. Geckos lay one or two eggs with soft, sticky shells. They often hide the eggs under tree bark until the shells harden. The young geckos take several months to develop inside the eggs. Eventually, they break their way out by using the pointed egg tooth on their snout.

The eyes have a fixed, transparent covering.

These mottled colours disguise the gecko against the bark and leaves in the forest.

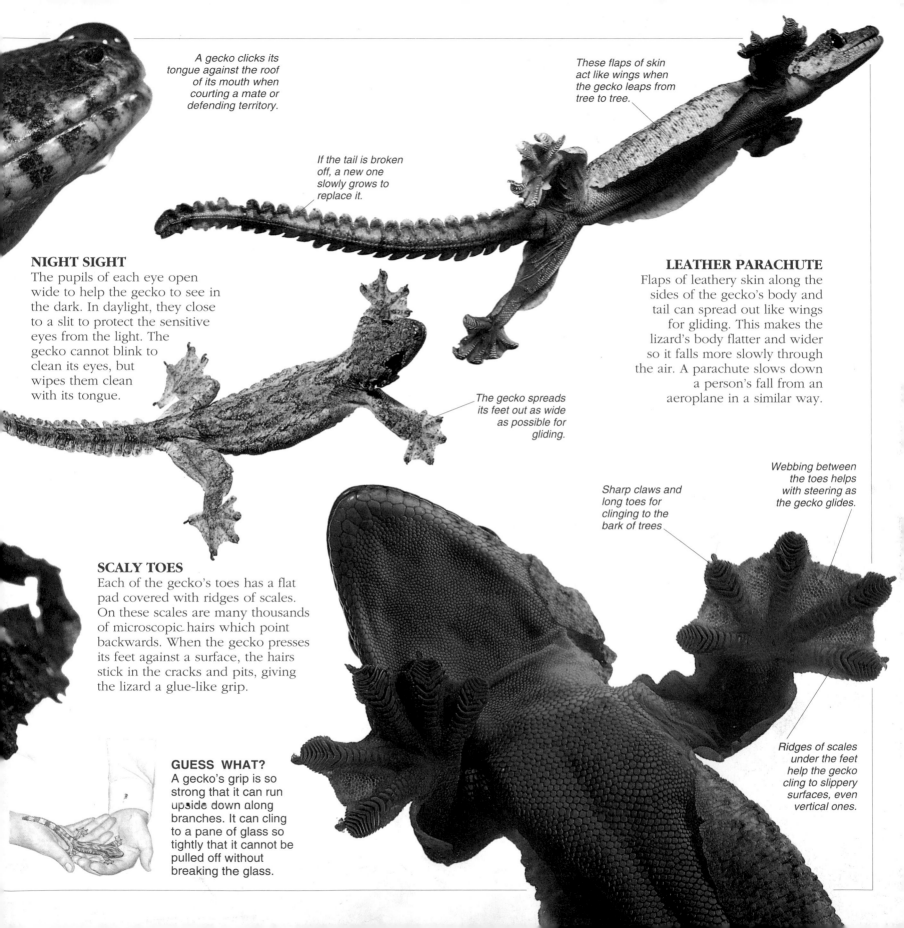

A gecko clicks its tongue against the roof of its mouth when courting a mate or defending territory.

These flaps of skin act like wings when the gecko leaps from tree to tree.

If the tail is broken off, a new one slowly grows to replace it.

NIGHT SIGHT
The pupils of each eye open wide to help the gecko to see in the dark. In daylight, they close to a slit to protect the sensitive eyes from the light. The gecko cannot blink to clean its eyes, but wipes them clean with its tongue.

LEATHER PARACHUTE
Flaps of leathery skin along the sides of the gecko's body and tail can spread out like wings for gliding. This makes the lizard's body flatter and wider so it falls more slowly through the air. A parachute slows down a person's fall from an aeroplane in a similar way.

The gecko spreads its feet out as wide as possible for gliding.

Webbing between the toes helps with steering as the gecko glides.

Sharp claws and long toes for clinging to the bark of trees

SCALY TOES
Each of the gecko's toes has a flat pad covered with ridges of scales. On these scales are many thousands of microscopic hairs which point backwards. When the gecko presses its feet against a surface, the hairs stick in the cracks and pits, giving the lizard a glue-like grip.

Ridges of scales under the feet help the gecko cling to slippery surfaces, even vertical ones.

GUESS WHAT?
A gecko's grip is so strong that it can run upside down along branches. It can cling to a pane of glass so tightly that it cannot be pulled off without breaking the glass.

MURDER BY POISON

LARGE POISONOUS CENTIPEDES scurry across the floor of the rainforest searching for prey. They feed mainly on insects and spiders but also catch small toads, snakes, and mammals. Their poison fangs are formidable weapons. Giant tiger centipedes like this one can easily dry out, so they come out only at night when the forest is cool and damp. During the day, the tiger centipede hides under leaves, logs, and bark where the air is moist. The female digs a hole in the earth under a stone and lays her eggs there. She curls her long body around the eggs to protect them. When they hatch, the young centipedes have just as many legs as their parents. They have to moult (shed their skin) in order to grow, because their hard outer skin, called the exoskeleton, will not stretch as they grow bigger.

Two long, jointed antennae help the centipede to feel its way around and detect food.

Mouthparts for tearing up food

On the end of the poison fang there is a curved claw that injects poison into a victim.

FEARSOME FANGS
Centipedes stun their prey with the large poison claws just below the head. They hold the victim firmly in their fangs and tear it to pieces with their mouthparts. The centipede eats only the soft parts of its prey.

Close-up, you can see tiny creatures called mites which live on the centipede.

There are four simple eyes on each side of the head.

Each poison fang has four sections.

LOADS OF LEGS
With its many long legs and flattened body, the centipede can run quickly and smoothly over, under, and around the plants of the rainforest. The legs lift the body off the ground so that it does not catch against leaves or twigs. Tiger centipedes can have up to 23 pairs of legs.

GUESS WHAT?
Giant tiger centipedes can give humans a very painful bite, rather like a hornet sting. But their poison is not normally dangerous.

TOXIC TIGER
Vivid orange and black tiger stripes on the tiger centipede's body warn enemies that it is poisonous. Predators soon learn to leave it alone.

The legs are attached to the sides of the body.

These jointed legs bend easily.

Each segment of the body has one breathing hole, called a spiracle.

Claws on the ends of the legs for gripping on to trees and rocks

Two large legs at the end of the abdomen help the centipede to hold its prey still while injecting poison into it.

A hard exoskeleton outside the body for protection

The bright colours warn other animals that the centipede is poisonous.

GLUED TO THE SPOT

THE DAMP, SHADY RAINFOREST makes an ideal home for frogs. They need to live in moist places because their skin is not waterproof and it dries out quickly. Frogs also need pools of water for their tadpoles to live in while they grow into adults. In the rainforest, some frogs lay their eggs on a leaf or a patch of ground which they have carefully cleared. When the tadpoles of poison dart frogs hatch out, they wriggle on to one of their parent's backs. The adult frog carries them to a pool of water in the centre of the leaves of plants called bromeliads. Tree frogs and poison dart frogs have large, sticky suckers on their fingers and toes. The suckers help them to cling on to smooth, wet leaves and mossy branches. Tree frogs can cling upside-down in the forest for hours on end.

FLABBY FROG
White's tree frogs are often very fat, with folds of flesh on their bodies. The skin on their bellies is loose and helps the frogs to grip as they climb up slippery tree trunks. Many tree frogs are green or brown to help them blend in with the colours of the forest and hide from enemies. Tree frogs usually hide by day and come out only at night.

Two large eyes allow the frog to see well both in daylight and at night when it hunts for food.

A wide mouth with a sticky tongue inside for catching beetles, moths, and other insects

The skin on the throat can expand like a balloon to make the frog's mating call louder.

These long, thin toes curl around leaves and twigs for extra grip.

Whenever the frog blinks, its eyelids move across the eyes to wipe them clean.

There is an eardrum on each side of the head. The frog can hear a wide range of sounds.

A poison dart frog's brilliant warning colours may be yellow, red, green, or blue.

GUESS WHAT?
South American Indians use the poison from poison dart frogs to tip their hunting darts. White's tree frogs have such big appetites that they sometimes eat rats.

DON'T EAT ME
The brilliant colours of poison dart frogs show enemies that they are dangerous. These frogs have special glands in their skin which produce a deadly poison. The poison can paralyze a bird or monkey immediately so they soon learn to leave the frogs alone. The most deadly kind of dart frog contains enough poison to kill six people.

STICKY FEET
Each finger and toe has a pad on the underside. These pads produce a sticky substance called mucus. The sticky mucus helps the frog to grip wet leaves and other slimy surfaces. With their sticky feet, tree frogs can even climb up slippery tree trunks.

Sticky pads on each finger

EATING MACHINE

IT IS HARD TO BELIEVE that this pale, spiky postman caterpillar will change into a brightly coloured butterfly. A caterpillar is the feeding and growing stage in the life cycle of a butterfly. It hatches out of an egg, often eating its own egg shell. Then it chews its way through huge amounts of leaves. Every few days the caterpillar moults so that its body can grow larger. After about three weeks it stops eating and turns into a pupa, or chrysalis, which hangs on a silken thread under a leaf. It cannot eat or drink. Inside the pupa, the caterpillar's body breaks down into a liquid. From the liquid, the body of the butterfly forms, then it emerges from the pupa. This fantastic change, from caterpillar to butterfly, is called metamorphosis.

BREATHING TUBES

Like all insects, the caterpillar breathes through holes called spiracles along the sides of its body. These holes lead to a network of tubes called tracheae inside the body. In dry weather, the spiracles can close to stop water escaping from the body.

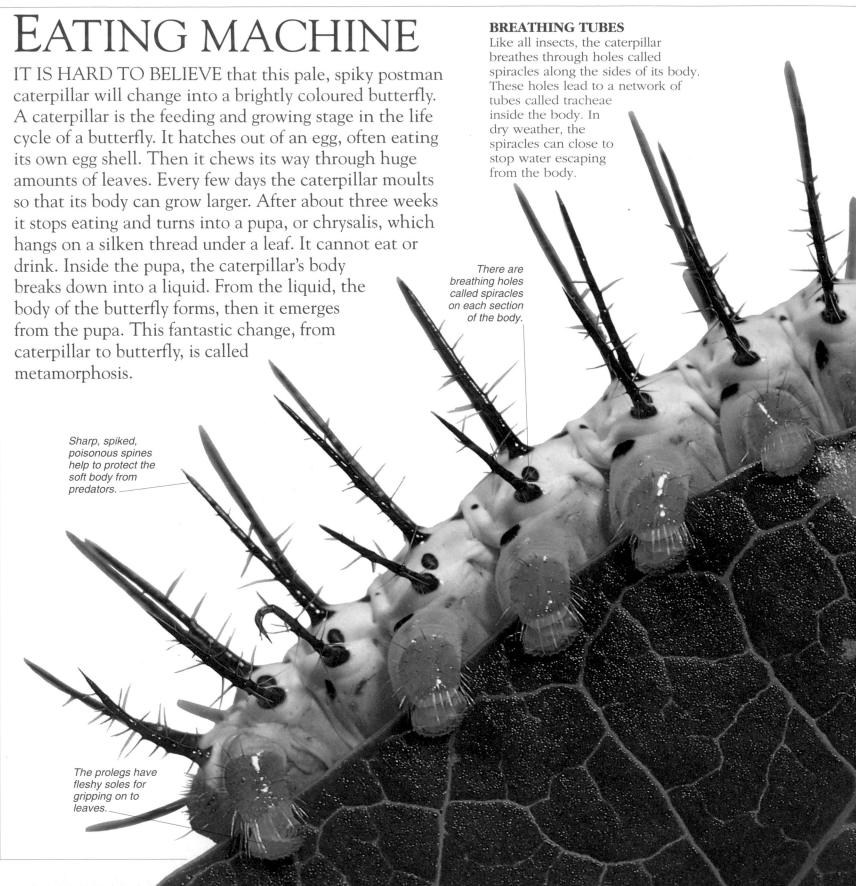

There are breathing holes called spiracles on each section of the body.

Sharp, spiked, poisonous spines help to protect the soft body from predators.

The prolegs have fleshy soles for gripping on to leaves.

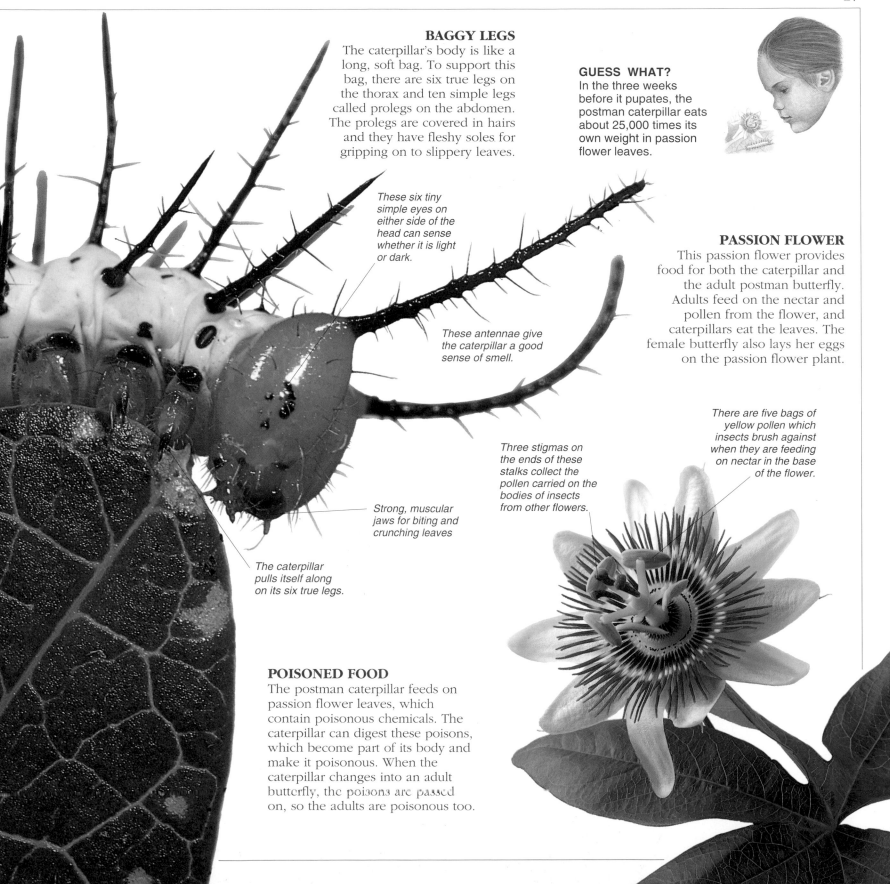

BAGGY LEGS

The caterpillar's body is like a long, soft bag. To support this bag, there are six true legs on the thorax and ten simple legs called prolegs on the abdomen. The prolegs are covered in hairs and they have fleshy soles for gripping on to slippery leaves.

GUESS WHAT?

In the three weeks before it pupates, the postman caterpillar eats about 25,000 times its own weight in passion flower leaves.

These six tiny simple eyes on either side of the head can sense whether it is light or dark.

These antennae give the caterpillar a good sense of smell.

PASSION FLOWER

This passion flower provides food for both the caterpillar and the adult postman butterfly. Adults feed on the nectar and pollen from the flower, and caterpillars eat the leaves. The female butterfly also lays her eggs on the passion flower plant.

There are five bags of yellow pollen which insects brush against when they are feeding on nectar in the base of the flower.

Three stigmas on the ends of these stalks collect the pollen carried on the bodies of insects from other flowers.

Strong, muscular jaws for biting and crunching leaves

The caterpillar pulls itself along on its six true legs.

POISONED FOOD

The postman caterpillar feeds on passion flower leaves, which contain poisonous chemicals. The caterpillar can digest these poisons, which become part of its body and make it poisonous. When the caterpillar changes into an adult butterfly, the poisons are passed on, so the adults are poisonous too.

CRUSHED VELVET

WHEN THIS POSTMAN butterfly pulls itself out of its pupa, its wings are soft, damp, and crushed. It takes about an hour for them to stretch and dry out. The main purpose in the life of adult butterflies is to find a mate and lay eggs. The male postman butterfly takes three months to mature before he can mate. The female lays 400 to 500 eggs because so many of the young caterpillars will be eaten by insects and spiders. She lays about 20 eggs at a time on the tender leaves and shoots of passion flower vines. She avoids plants with other eggs or caterpillars on them because caterpillars often eat each other.

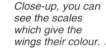

Close-up, you can see the scales which give the wings their colour.

GUESS WHAT?
Most butterflies live for only a few days or weeks. But postman butterflies live for up to nine months because they feed on pollen as well as nectar. Pollen is rich in nutrients, especially proteins.

SCALY WINGS
Each wing is covered with thousands of tiny, overlapping scales which give the wings their colour. Butterflies and moths belong to a group of insects called *Lepidoptera*, which means "scaled wing".

When it is not being used, the proboscis is curled up under the head, out of the way.

Six jointed legs are joined to the middle part of the body, called the thorax.

The proboscis is like a straw for sucking up liquid food.

Female postman butterflies lay their eggs on the leaves and shoots of the passion flower.

POLLEN SOUP
The postman butterfly feeds on nectar and pollen, using the long proboscis on its head. Before it can eat hard, dry pollen, the butterfly squirts a mixture of nectar and special fluids on to the pollen, turning it into a mushy soup. It sucks up this liquid through its long proboscis.

The compound eyes are good at detecting movement. Each one has thousands of separate lenses.

The antennae end in a club-shaped tip.

The black and red colouring warns enemies that the butterfly is poisonous.

Pollen from this blue passion flower is a good source of protein for the butterfly.

COLOUR MESSAGES
The black and red colours of the postman butterfly are common among poisonous insects. Birds quickly learn to avoid bright colours, and leave these butterflies alone. Postman butterflies do not need to fly fast because their warning colours protect them. They fly slowly and lazily high up in the rainforest canopy.

The butterfly's wings are very large compared to the size of its body.

FURRY FLYER

SHY, SECRETIVE FRUIT BATS leave the trees at dusk and fly over the rainforest canopy to search for food. They cannot turn well as they fly, and so prefer to avoid the thick plant growth lower down in the forest. Fruit bats feed mainly on fruits such as figs, mangoes, and bananas. They spit out seeds from these fruits, or pass them out in their droppings, and this helps the trees to spread throughout the forest. Many bats live in large groups, but male Franquet's fruit bats usually roost (sleep or rest) alone. The females sometimes roost in groups when they are nursing their young. Bats are blind and hairless when they are born. They cling on to their mother's fur, and drink her milk. After a few weeks, the young bats have fur too, and they start learning how to fly.

JUICE EXTRACTOR

Franquet's fruit bat sucks out the juices from rainforest fruits. It puts its lips around the fruit and bites into the flesh with its teeth. Then the bat squashes the fruit with its strong tongue.

The bat flexes these arm bones up and down to flap its wings.

GUESS WHAT?
This bat is also called the epauletted fruit bat. This is because the male has tufts of white fur on its shoulders, like the shoulder pieces (epaulettes) on a person's uniform.

The skin is tightly stretched between the bones so that the wings are both light and strong.

SKINNY WINGS
Bats are the only mammals that can fly. Their wings are made of an elastic membrane covered with skin. This is stretched between the four very long fingers on each hand. Bats lick their wings to keep them clean and in good condition for flying. On a hot day, they flap their wings like fans to keep themselves cool.

A fox-like face gives fruit bats the nickname of flying foxes.

Hearing is not very important for finding food, so the ears are small.

The jointed arms have elbows like ours, so that the bat can fold its wings away when resting.

Strong feet with claws for grasping branches and holding food

Fruit bats use their keen sense of smell to help them find fruit to eat.

Bats hang upside down to roost.

The claw at the tip of this finger is for clinging on to branches

SUPER SIGHT

Most bats have weak eyesight. Instead, they use their specially adapted hearing to find their way around and catch prey. But fruit bats like this one have excellent eyesight, so they do not need such good hearing as other bats. The fruit bat's sense of smell is also very good, and helps it to find the fruit that it likes to eat.

HAIRY HUNTER

THIS LARGE, HAIRY SPIDER is not as dangerous as it looks. The curly-haired tarantula can kill small rodents, reptiles, or birds, but its bite is usually no more dangerous to people than a bee or wasp sting. During the day, tarantulas lurk under stones, bark, or leaves, or inside their silk-lined burrows on the forest floor. At night, they come out to hunt. Curly-haired tarantulas feel for prey in the darkness with two leg-like pedipalps on the front of the body. Female tarantulas lay eggs, then cover them with a cocoon of silk for protection. The young spiderlings hatch inside the cocoon and emerge after they have moulted once. As they grow into adults, they moult several more times. Female tarantulas like this one also moult when they are adults.

Spinnerets at the end of the abdomen produce silk.

Each hair is shaped like a tiny harpoon with hooks along it. The hairs can cause itching and sneezing in other animals.

ITCHY HAIRS
The hairs on the tarantula's body can feel vibrations in the air. This helps the spider to find its way around and hunt in the dark. The hairs on its abdomen break off easily and irritate the skin of other animals, including humans. Tarantulas use their back legs to flick these hairs at enemies.

SPINNING SILK
At the end of the abdomen there are four spinnerets which the spider uses to spin silk. This silk is stronger than the same thickness of nylon rope or steel cable, and it is very stretchy.

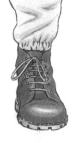

GUESS WHAT?
The curly-haired tarantula is not a true tarantula, despite its name. It belongs to a family of spiders called bird-eating spiders.

The body consists of two parts with a narrow waist, called a pedicel, in the middle.

Each leg is made up of seven parts, with two claws at the end and a tuft of hair underneath for extra grip.

POISON FANGS

Tarantulas are strong spiders. They pounce on their prey and hold it still with their pedipalps while their fangs inject poison. The poison paralyzes the prey and a special fluid from the spider's stomach digests the soft parts. The spider then sucks up the contents of its victim's body.

The eight simple eyes are tiny, so the spider can see very little.

Pedipalps look like extra legs.

Huge fangs for injecting prey with poison

THE HIGH LIFE

THESE RAINFOREST ORCHIDS perch high on the branches of the tallest trees, where they are close to the sunlight. Plants which grow on trees and other plants without harming them are called epiphytes. These orchids have long, trailing roots to soak up moisture from the air. They also store food and water in swollen stems called pseudobulbs. Their colourful, scented flowers attract insects. The insects eat the nectar made by the flower, and carry its pollen to other orchids. If an orchid flower receives pollen from another of the same kind, seeds may develop. Orchids produce thousands of tiny seeds which travel through the forest on the wind. If they land in a suitable spot, they grow into new plants.

The clusters of pollen called pollinia are near the top of the flower.

POLLEN PARCELS
Most flowers have loose, dust-like pollen. But orchids have special clusters called pollinia consisting of thousands of pollen grains. Each cluster has a special pad at its base. This sticks to the head of a visiting insect, which carries it to another orchid flower.

Below the pollinia is the stigma (the tip of the female part).

The labellum of this flower forms a flat landing platform for insects.

Brightly coloured petals to attract insects

FANTASTIC FLOWER
Orchids have unusual flowers. The stem of the male part (the stamen) and the stem of the female part (the style) are joined together in a central column. One of the orchid's petals, called the labellum, is a special shape, to attract the right kind of insect. The insect cannot get to the nectar it feeds on without becoming covered in pollen.

The flat, green leaves use sunlight to produce food for the plant.

There is a tough, waxy surface on each leaf to cut down water loss.

Each flower has three petals and three sepals. The sepals are longer and narrower than the petals.

STRONG SCENTS

In the rainforest, the light is dim. To help attract the insects which pollinate them, orchids often have a very strong scent. These orchids have sweet, heavy perfumes. Others smell of rotting meat, depending on the insects they need to attract.

GUESS WHAT?

There are more than 25,000 kinds of orchids in the world. Three quarters of these live by perching on other plants. A single orchid plant may produce up to one million seeds.

GLOSSARY

Abdomen *the rear part of the body*
Antennae *a pair of feelers*
Cocoon *a bag which an insect larva makes from silk when it is ready to pupate*
Exoskeleton *a protective outer covering on the body, made of a hard substance called chitin*
Fang *a large, pointed tooth*
Labellum *part of an orchid flower, often shaped like a lip*
Larvae *grubs, which eventually develop into adult insects*
Mammal *a warm-blooded animal such as a mouse or a rabbit*
Metamorphosis *a complete change of appearance*

Moult *to shed the skin or exoskeleton*
Mucus *a slimy, often poisonous substance which certain animals produce*
Pedipalps *the leg-like parts on a spider's head*
Proboscis *the long, straw-like mouthpart of a butterfly or moth*
Pupa/chrysalis *the resting stage between a larva and an adult insect*
Roost *to rest or sleep, often in a high place*
Sepals *the outer parts of a flower which protect the bud*
Thorax *the front part of the body*
Trachea *a windpipe, for breathing*
Vibrations *tiny movements in air, in water, or underground*